Improving Your
LOVE
LIFE

by
Norman Robertson

Improving Your
LOVE
LIFE

by

Norman Robertson

NRM Publications
P.O. Box 10310
Charlotte, North Carolina 28212

Improving Your Love Life
ISBN 0-9636898-1-9
Copyright © 1994 by
Norman Robertson
P.O. Box 10310
Charlotte, NC 28212

Published by NRM Publications
P.O. Box 10310
Charlotte, NC 28212

DEDICATION

To my wonderful Lord and Savior, Jesus Christ for His immeasurable love towards me – a love so abundant it surpasses human understanding and beggars description.

All I can say is these few simple words: "Thank you Lord Jesus for loving me before the foundation of the world!" (1 John 4:10,11)

CONTENTS

I

INTRODUCTION: FOLLOWING IN THE FOOTSTEPS OF JESUS

Therefore be followers of God as dear children.
And walk in love, as Christ also has loved us and given
Himself for us, an offering and a sacrifice to God for a sweet-
smelling aroma.

Ephesians 5:1,2

The characteristic of *love*, a fruit of the Spirit (Gal. 5:22,23), has been secularized, cheapened, merchandized, and stereotyped in this generation. The problem is not just in the world. Many Christians do not really understand what "walking in love" means. It sounds good. The phrase rolls off the tongue so easily that we think we know what it means. Yet most of us do not.

I once heard a renowned minister who I greatly respect say that Christians should not preach or teach something until they have tried it out in their own lives long enough to *know* that it works. In other words, "practice what you preach" before you preach it. He says that he has done that with every revelation or insight the Lord has brought to him over the years.

Before being led by the Holy Spirit to publish this book, I was "tested" by circumstances until I can truly say that I *know* what walking in love means. I know that it is a choice, not an emotion. I know that it is something I do whether I "feel" like it or whether I don't "feel" like it.

I try to make choices because they are the right choices, the ones Jesus Himself would make in the same situation if He were still walking on earth as a man. We see in the life of Jesus that He never spoke a word of condemnation or self-defense, although the pain and anguish of being crucified by those He loved better than life itself must have been almost unbearable.

In a manner of speaking, He *is* still walking on earth through men and women. He dwells within His Body, the Church, in the Person of the Holy Spirit. When we do not act as Jesus would, we grieve the Holy Spirit and belittle Jesus' sacrifice on the cross. We should not only accept Jesus in our hearts, but we should reflect Jesus in our lives as well.

Religious Politics

My heart has been saddened many times over the years, while traveling through the Body of Christ as a Bible teacher and evangelist, by ministers who preach "walking in love," but who do not walk in it themselves. Too often, strife, division, and religious politics undermine the effectiveness of pastors and weaken the anointing among ministries and churches today.

For the past five years, I have ministered in South Africa, Europe, and the United States. Just in that period of time, I have been in hundreds of churches and seen many things go on that hinder the advancement of God's Kingdom. These things are done in the interest of building or maintaining someone's personal "kingdom" at the expense of God's Kingdom. A lot of pastors are little "empire builders" and are not building the Kingdom of God.

Jealousy, envy, backbiting, and competition are still sins whether sinners do them or Christians. There will never be real unity in the Body until the leaders in five-fold offices learn to truly "prefer" one another. (Rom. 12:10.)

In some places, I have been told by pastors, "If you speak at so-and-so's church, I will not have you back at my church."

I have heard other pastors comparing their churches to other churches in their towns in terms of the "numbers game":

"How big is *your* church? How many are you running?"

I have seen so-called successful pastors with large churches look down their noses at pastors of smaller churches. And the same situation exists with evangelists, who sometimes brag about the size of their meetings as compared to the meetings of others.

Is it any wonder so many churches today have dried up and become dead with no moving of the Holy Spirit in evidence? A church can be dead even with thousands of members. It can have degenerated into a social club where the community leaders attend as part of their civic duties and hear nice little "pep" talks or lectures on Sunday mornings.

The Holy Spirit is not going to bless pastors with critical spirits, or those who are full of jealousy, pride, and ambition – at least not in these days of revival when God is sending a fresh outpouring of His Spirit just before the return of Jesus.

If someone says, "I love God," and hates his brother, he is a liar; for he who does not love his brother whom he has seen, how can he love God whom he has not seen?
And this commandment we have from Him: that he who loves God must love his brother also.
1 John 4:20,21

Love Will Be Tested

Perhaps the biggest test I have had of "walking in love" occurred after we moved to the United States. When my wife, Eleanor, our two children, and I left South Africa at the leading of the Holy Spirit, we virtually had to begin our lives all over again. We sold most of what we owned to raise funds for the move, just legal fees alone for this kind of move are thousands of dollars.

In order for us to comply with regulations of the U.S. Department of Immigration, we had to be sponsored by a local church in the United States. We talked with the pastor of a church where I had ministered several times as guest speaker about moving to America, and he wholeheartedly agreed to sponsor us. So we came to the United States and moved into an apartment.

Initially, things went very well at the church where we moved. I was hired as a minister on staff and established a six-month laymen's Bible training school at the church while continuing with my traveling ministry on weekends.

During this same period of time, the pastor asked me to take the Sunday services once a month, and these services were successful in the sense that attendance increased and many lives were touched by God through healings, salvations, and baptisms in the Holy Spirit. The laymen's Bible school seemed to be especially blessed by God, transforming many lives. My traveling ministry began to expand across the United States.

What I somehow overlooked in those first few months was that the pastor of our home church was becoming increasingly insecure in face of the fact that God was blessing my teaching ministry. An attitude of competition, jealousy, and insecurity is deadly, whether it is a "King Saul" fearful of his own position or an "Absalom" trying to usurp authority. Both are two sides of the same coin.

We had been in the United States nine months and were just six weeks away from the finalization of our "green cards" (the permits that enable us to live here permanently) when I went on a two-week ministry trip to England. While I was gone, the pastor – without a word of warning to us – contacted the U.S. Department of Immigration and withdrew his sponsorship.

We were left "high and dry" in trouble with the federal government and with the loss of $5,000 in legal fees. We had to begin all over again with new fees, new applications, and a new sponsor in order to be able to remain in the United States.

You can imagine how hurt, angry, and upset my wife and I were. This pastor not only had broken his promise to us, but without a word of communication, he had gone behind our backs and almost gotten us deported! In the natural, my flesh wanted to confront him.

However, as my wife and I prayed, the Lord told us to "walk in love" and forgive the man. Then He would take care of us.

I know, you see, from personal experience that "walking in love" is sometimes an extremely hard choice to make. However, I also knew that I could forgive the man by acting on God's Word. (Mark 11:25,26.) I did not have to "feel" loving toward him before forgiving him.

Forgiveness is a choice, not an emotion! The peace of love in one's heart will come after choices are made. If you wait for the feeling to come so that you *want* to forgive, you will never do it.

With the help of the Holy Spirit, we were able to live out our decision, and today, I can say that we have no hard feelings toward this man whatsoever. Because of two very good ministry friends, who helped us and stood by us through this entire trying episode, we were able to start over. God opened up to us an alternative way to make our home in the United States.

We had to forgive this pastor and trust God to bring us victory in the face of apparent defeat. He called us here, so we knew He would make a way for us to stay if we did not hinder Him with our own attitudes.

I am convinced that if we had reacted in a fleshly way toward this pastor, we would not be in the position of blessing that we are in today. The Apostle Paul wrote that "love *never* fails." (1 Cor. 13:8.)

Honor the Holy Spirit

For the Church of Jesus Christ to accomplish God's will in this hour, every leader who wants to be part of what the Holy Spirit is doing must deal with the spirit of competition and give no place to the devil through envy, jealousy, insecurity, or a critical tongue. The Bible calls such activities the works of the flesh and spiritual cannibalism! (Gal. 5:15-21.) Yielding to the flesh always grieves and dishonors the Holy Spirit. (Eph. 4:29,30).

I call ministers and laymen alike to love one another and build the Kingdom of God in a spirit of togetherness, love, and unity.

Let us begin to pull down the walls of division, competition, and critical attitudes. Let us honor the Holy Spirit by putting on the Christlike spirit and following the way of love.

> **The ultimate aim of the Christian ministry, after all, is to produce the love which springs from a pure heart, a good conscience, and a genuine faith.**
>
> 1 Timothy 1:5 PHI

Key Thought: Walking in love is the highest spiritual force, and will keep you in harmony with God and man.

1

IMPROVING YOUR LOVE LIFE

Therefore, if anyone is in Christ, he is a new creation; old things have passed away; behold, all things have become new.

2 Corinthians 5:17

Nearly every person would like his, or her, love life to improve. However, most people would immediately think of "improving one's love life" in terms of the physical realm. Even many Christians would tend to think first of natural relationships.

The Word of God makes it plain to us that the most important "love life" a Christian has must center in our Lord and Savior, Jesus Christ. Without the depth of a true love life founded on Jesus, even our physical relationships are empty and meaningless. It is easy to see this played out before our eyes in the present condition of American society: divorce, crime, abortion, and all of the other ills that go with a self-centered and faithless generation.

The children of God have no excuse for living loveless lives like the children of the world. The Apostle Paul wrote that we become "new creations" (2 Cor. 5:17) once we are born again into the Kingdom of God. That means we have within us the characteristics of our Father.

God Is Love

Beloved, let us love one another, for love is of God; and everyone who loves is born of God and knows God.

He who does not love does not know God, for God is love.

1 John 4:7,8

15

The basic characteristic of God's nature is love.

The Bible says that God *is* love and that He "so loved the world" that He sent His beloved Son to live as a man in a fallen world surrounded by beings with "human" natures instead of the God-natures with which Adam and Eve were created. The whole mission of Jesus Christ coming to this earth was a "love mission" to redeem lost mankind by dying unselfishly on the cross reconciling man back to God. (John 3:16.)

The basic characteristic of human nature is self.

God loved us while we were still sinners, Paul wrote. (Eph. 2:4,5.) It is not possible while in our natural state to fully understand the love of God. However, we can *believe* it and accept it. Galatians 5:22,23 lists the nine fruit of the Holy Spirit, which are to be the fruit of our new creation nature:

> **But the fruit of the Spirit is love, joy, peace, longsuffering, kindness, goodness, faithfulness,**
> **Gentleness, self-control. Against such there is no law.**

Love is listed as first of the nine fruit, and that is important because without love, none of the others are possible. The other eight are all facets of love. It is as if *love* is the tree or root from which all of the others spring.

Love Is a Fruit

The fruit of the Spirit is the *character* of Christ produced by the *Spirit* of Christ in the *follower* of Christ. Love is a fruit. There is no such thing as "the gift of love," the "baptism of love," the "anointing of love," or praying for love.

> **For the whole Law [concerning human relationships] is complied with in the one precept, You shall love your neighbor as [you do] yourself.**
>
> **Galatians 5:14 AMP**

The Apostle Paul wrote that *all* of the Law is summed up in, or compiled within, one principle: loving others as much as you do yourself. Love is the ultimate test for being a true disciple of Christ. (John 13:35.)

Actually, Paul was repeating something Jesus had said:

"A new commandment I give to you, that you love one another; as I have loved you, that you also love one another.

"By this all will know that you are My disciples, if you have love for one another."

John 13:34,35

Since Jesus' resurrection, the Law has been written on the hearts of those born again into the Kingdom of God under the New Covenant, not on tablets of stone. (Heb. 10:16.) So the hearts of God's people should love Him and then let His love flow out of them.

"'You shall love the Lord your God with all your heart, with all your soul, and with all your mind.'

"This is the first and great commandment.

"And the second is like it: 'You shall love your neighbor as yourself.'

"On these two commandments hang all the Law and the Prophets."

Matthew 22:37-40

Under the inspiration of the Holy Spirit, Paul wrote that **the old has gone** and **the new has come** (2 Cor. 5:17 NIV). The problem is that most Christians do not act as if this is true. They are new on the inside but act like the same old creature on the outside.

Allowing this new creation nature to permeate one's whole life is a process. First, we must learn what, or rather *Who*, the new person is like – Jesus. Then we must begin to talk, walk, and act like Him. This process becomes a reality as we daily depend upon the Holy Spirit and renew our thinking with God's Word.

New Creation Truths

To walk this love walk, there are four basic truths you should know as a new creation in Christ.

1. As a new creation, you should know that you are a partaker of God's divine nature and personality.

The truth is that he who is born again possesses the nature of God and, by *nature*, is a lover not a fighter.

By which have been given to us exceedingly great and precious promises, that through these you may be partakers of the divine nature, having escaped the corruption that is in the world through lust.

2 Peter 1:4

2. As a new creation, you should know that when you were born again, you received the *spirit of love*.

For God has not given us a spirit of fear, but of power and of love and of a sound mind.

2 Timothy 1:7

God has given every born-again believer many things through the Holy Spirit. According to that verse, here are three of them:

- Power

- Love

- A sound mind

The power, of course, is ours when we are filled with the Holy Spirit. Jesus promised us that. (Acts 1:8.)

Unless we are walking in love, we are operating in an "unsound" mind! Walking in the same old nature we had before we received Jesus is like having a million-dollar budget placed at our disposal, but choosing to live on the same old hundred-dollar budget we used to have.

The human tongue can be the greatest hindrance to walking in love. If all Christians would obey Paul's instructions to the Ephesians, their speech would not get in the way of love.

Let no foul or polluting language, nor evil word nor unwholesome or worthless talk [ever] come out of your mouth, but only such [speech] as is good and beneficial to the spiritual progress of others, as is fitting to the need and

the occasion, that it may be a blessing and give grace (God's favor) to those who hear it.

Ephesians 4:29 AMP

In your daily conversation, on the telephone, in meeting people, *before* opening your mouth at all, ask yourself these questions about what you are going to say:

- Is it true?

- Is it kind?

- Is it helpful and constructive?

- Is it edifying? Does it build up or tear down?

If what you are about to say lacks truth in some area, then you need to check your motives. Ask yourself why you were going to say something not quite true. Was it to gain approval, or to get attention? Was it to get even with someone (retaliation), or to "take someone down a peg"?

If what you are about to say is not kind, remember that it is not necessary to tell everything you know.

If what you are about to say is not going to help someone, it would be better not to say it or else rephrase it in a more helpful way.

If what you are about to say tears down someone instead of building them up, you certainly should not say it!

3. As a new creation, you should know that the Holy Spirit has poured the divine love of God into your heart.

And hope does not disappoint us, because God has poured out His love into our hearts (not our heads and not our flesh) **by the Holy Spirit, whom He has given us.**

Romans 5:5 NIV

God's love produced in the heart by the Holy Spirit is an unselfish love that motivates a person to deny himself for the sake of loving others. Love always is ready to believe the best of every person, not the worst. (Gal. 5:14-16.)

4. As a new creation, the fourth thing you should know is that being born again should release the Christlike personality within you – in other words people should be able to see Jesus in you.

As you mature in your Christian walk, you are to show forth the fruit of the Spirit, and if these fruits are not manifesting in your life, you need to check your "love thermometer," which is found in 1 Corinthians 13:4-8 (AMP):

> Love endures long and is patient and kind; love never is envious nor boils over with jealousy, is not boastful or vainglorious, does not display itself haughtily.
>
> It is not conceited (arrogant and inflated with pride); it is not rude (unmannerly) and does not act unbecomingly. Love (God's love in us) does not insist on its own rights or its own way, for it is not self-seeking; it is not touchy or fretful or resentful; it takes no account of the evil done to it [pays no attention to a suffered wrong].
>
> It does not rejoice at injustice and unrighteousness, but rejoices when right and truth prevail.
>
> Love bears up under anything and everything that comes, is ever ready to believe the best of every person, its hopes are fadeless under all circumstances, and it endures everything [without weakening].
>
> Love never fails [never fades out or becomes obsolete or comes to an end]. As for prophecy (the gift of interpreting the divine will and purpose), it will be fulfilled and pass away; as for tongues, they will be destroyed and cease; as for knowledge, it will pass away [it will lose its value and be superseded by truth].

Are You a Noisy Gong?

So often our Christian lives reflect a lack of walking in love, and according to Paul, this produces a three-fold negative result in our lives:

Firstly, without love, God's Word says we are "clanging cymbals." In other words, we make a lot of noise, but no music. The Greek literally means "a noisy gong."

Though I speak with the tongues of men and of angels, but have not love, I have become as sounding brass or a clanging cymbal.

1 Corinthians 13:1

Secondly, without love flowing out to others, we are useless to ourselves and to others.

And though I have the gift of prophecy, and understand all mysteries and all knowledge, and though I have all faith, so that I could remove mountains, but have not love, I am nothing.

1 Corinthians 13:2

Thirdly, without showing forth the love of God within us, we achieve nothing.

And though I bestow all my goods to feed the poor, and though I give my body to be burned, but have not love, it profits me nothing.

1 Corinthians 13:3

Paul said the best minister, the best preacher or evangelist or Bible teacher, or the best orator might as well not speak or minister if he does not do it with, and through, the love of God.

The Royal Law of the New Covenant

The law of love is the royal law of the New Covenant, the supreme and highest law. (Matt. 22:36-40.)

If indeed you [really] fulfill the royal Law in accordance with the Scripture, You shall love your neighbor as [you love] yourself, you do well.

James 2:8 AMP

The phrase "royal law" means:

(a) The ruling, superior, ultimate law of life.

(b) The foundation law, or controlling principle, on which all the rest of the laws of life rest and operate.

In James 2:8, the word *well* means "to be happy, healthy, and prosperous." For a Christian to be "well," he must fulfill the royal law, which has three levels:

21

Number One: *Love the Lord first.* (Matt. 6:33.)

You must maintain proper priorities in your life. God comes first, then your family, and after that your local church; next comes your job/business/career, with social activities last. When these priorities get mixed up, your life will become progressively confused and chaotic until you end up "stressed out."

Number Two: *Love yourself.*

You must have a godly self-esteem, a healthy, positive, Biblical self-image. Begin to ask the Holy Spirit to show you yourself as God sees you. Realize you are valuable and precious to God. Your Heavenly Father loves you so much that if you were the only person on earth, He would still have sent His Son Jesus to the cross so that you could receive eternal life.

You are special to God. He has no one else in His family exactly like you. You are unique *in Christ,* not because of your natural self, but because you are His workmanship. It is vital that you see yourself the way God sees you, and that you start loving yourself!

How can you reach out to love other people and show them the love of God, if you dislike, hate, or reject yourself?

Number Three: *Love and serve your fellow man.*

Decide you are going to be a blessing to those around you. Love brings out the best in other people. The fruit of selfishness or self-centeredness is fear, which leads to hatred and rejection of others. (1 John 4:18.)

Selfishness is the foundation of fear.

Love is the foundation of faith.

Jesus was able to love the unlovable, because He controlled His emotions. *Love is not an emotion.* Jesus knew that love dwelled inside of Him, and He chose to show forth the Father through love rather than let His emotions rule. Jesus constantly walked in the love of God, loving the unlovely, and reaching out to meet people's needs. Jesus was committed to loving others — not because of His emotions but because of a quality decision which He had made.

Emotions, or feelings, will change from minute to minute, but *love never changes*. The problem most Christians face after being born again is learning to control their emotional reactions to things other people do or say. Instead of seeing that their enemy really is the devil, they treat things done or said to them as personal attacks. Then they strike back, putting themselves on the same level as the people who offended them. This is totally unproductive, a "no-win situation."

God's love, which abides in you, can overlook things said and done to you; human love cannot.

Key Thought: Love is a commandment, not an option for the Christian.

2

WHAT DOES LOVE MEAN TO YOU?

This love of which I speak is slow to lose patience — it looks for a way of being constructive. It is not possessive; it is neither anxious to impress nor does it cherish inflated ideas of its own importance.

Love has good manners and does not pursue selfish advantage.

It is not touchy. It does not keep account of evil or gloat over the wickedness of other people. On the contrary, it shares the joy of those who live by the truth.

Love knows no limit to its endurance, no end to its trust, no fading of its hope; it can outlast anything.

Love never fails.

1 Corinthians 13:4-8 PHI

Did you know that the word *love* means different things to different people?

In today's Western society, love often is a shallow, superficial, surface-type of emotion. In English, we use the word to mean "like," "need," or "want":

I love classical music.

I love T-bone steaks.

I love chocolate ice cream.

I love cats.

I love apple pie.

I love sailing.

We confuse sexual love with real love.

"I love you, honey," can mean, "I want to have an affair with you"; or, it can mean a true, life-long bonding of two people in a true marriage.

We even use "love" when we mean "wish."

"I would love to be able to preach like that," or sing, or write, or whatever. That is a desire, a wish, not "love."

When we say, "I love You, Jesus," it may be simply a sudden burst of emotion from a good praise and worship service. Jesus said that if we truly loved Him, we would do His commandments.

This is My commandment, that you love one another as I have loved you.

Greater love has no one than this, than to lay down one's life for his friends.

John 15:12,13

Jesus told Peter, "If you love Me, feed My sheep." (John 21:15-17.)

In other words, love is an action as we saw in the last chapter.

What is *your* understanding of love?

Does love to you mean, "I will love you if you meet my needs?"

Does love to you mean, "I will love this person as long as things run smoothly?"

Does your love of God mean, "I will love Him as long as He keeps blessing and prospering me?"

God may say to you some day, "Are you going to love Me and serve Me because of *Who* I am, or because of what I can do for you?"

Walking in the Love of God

By this we know love, because He laid down His life for us. And we also ought to lay down our lives for the brethren.

But whoever has this world's goods, and sees his brother in need, and shuts up his heart from him, how does the love of God abide in him?

My little children, let us not love in word or in tongue, but in deed and in truth.

1 John 3:16-18

I believe that the majority of people in the world today really do *not* understand what real love is! The proof is in the number of broken homes and families, battered wives and abused children, millions of abortions, and uncounted millions of teenagers lost and in trouble. That is why it is vital for Christians to practice authentic, real love that is taught in the New Testament. When we begin to live and operate in the God-kind of love, it releases positive results in our lives.

Three positive results of walking in love are:

- Your faith will function effectively. (Gal. 5:6.)

- Love causes all fear to be removed from your life. (1 John 4:18.)

- Love causes you to be filled with the fullness of God. (Eph. 3:19.)

It is possible to walk in the love of God to the point that your whole being is saturated with love.

It is possible to walk so in the love of God that every word you speak drips with love, and everyone you come into contact with is affected by that love.

Now hope does not disappoint, because the love of God has been poured out in our hearts by the Holy Spirit who was given to us.

Romans 5:5

When we are full of, and controlled by, the Holy Spirit, we will manifest the love of God in our everyday lives. I have set myself to be completely Holy Spirit-possessed. I intend for Him to totally, completely, and absolutely operate in my life. It is my will that He do that!

I am not submitting to Him to do only the things I want or even in obedience to do the things I do not want to do.

I am submitting to Him to do whatever He desires in any way and at any time that He desires.

The Fruit of the Natural Man

We looked at the fruit of the Spirit in the last chapter. Let's look at the opposite: the fruit of the natural man. Among these are:

- Selfishness, or self-centeredness

- Pride

- Jealousy and envy

- Fear

- Hatred

- Bitterness and resentment

- Impatience and frustration

The natural man wants his own way no matter what the cost to others. He does not want to submit to authority, and says things like this:

"I hate him."

"I'll get even one day!"

"I never want to see him again."

Having these kinds of attitudes and speaking in this manner reveals the natural fleshly man dominating your life

And do not grieve the Holy Spirit of God, by whom you were sealed for the day of redemption.

Let all bitterness, wrath, anger, clamor, and evil speaking be put away from you, with all malice.

And be kind to one another, tenderhearted, forgiving one another, just as God in Christ also forgave you.

Ephesians 4:30-32

The Love of Christ Constrains Us

I heard Brother Kenneth Hagin share his experience about growing up in a broken home with a "chip on his shoulder." Because of a heart condition, he could not fight like his older brother. But, if someone talked about him or did something to him, he would never speak to that person again.

He would "mark them off his list" even to the extent of crossing the street to keep from meeting them. Not long after he was born again and healed of fatal diseases at the age of 17, one of his relatives did something to him.

His first reaction was out of the "old nature," or what Paul called "the old man." (Eph. 4:22-24.) He decided not to speak to, or have anything to do with, that person again. The very next day as he walked in the business district of his hometown, he saw this person coming toward him. So he started to cross the street and ignore this relative.

Then "something" rose up inside him.

It was the *love of Christ constraining* him. (2 Cor. 5:14.)

He realized that he *had* the love of God inside of him. He did not have to walk in the flesh or let those old attitudes dominate him. Nor did he have to "feel" like forgiving. He could *choose* to let the love of God flow through him to his relative.

Brother Hagin put action to his love, went to meet this person in the middle of the street, and took the initiative. He grabbed that person's hand, shook it, and expressed his love.

He even said, with tears in his eyes, "I'm praying for you, and if it would help any, I would get down right here on the street and kiss your feet."

Imagine a 17-year-old having that kind of revelation of what the love of God means! Many Christians much older could not do that today.

Of course, the other person burst into tears and asked Hagin's forgiveness.

Natural love cannot do this kind of thing.

Human love and God's love are exact opposites.

Human Love Is Bankrupt

Human love is selfish, while divine love is unselfish.

Human love is conditional, while real love is unconditional.

Human love is based on performance, while real love is never based on what another person does for, or to, you.

Human love is really not love at all, but emotions and carnal feelings, while real love has no carnal feelings.

Human love is self-seeking, while true love is self-giving.

Human love demands its own way, while true love puts other people first.

Human love holds grudges and retaliates, while real love walks in forgiveness and refuses to be offended.

Human love can change in a minute when jealousy, envy, or competitiveness intervenes, while real love (divine love) enjoys helping others succeed and rejoices when others get blessed.

Human love says, "I want to be seen; I want recognition."

Human love likes to brag and boast about "me, myself, and I," while real love walks in humility and builds up others.

Human love can criticize, judge, and find fault, changing with the emotional "weather," while real love overlooks people's faults and believes the best of every person. (1 Cor. 13:7 AMP.)

Human love is full of self-importance and seeks personal gain or advantage even at someone else's disadvantage, while real love lifts people up to one's own hurt.

Let nothing be done through selfish ambition or conceit, but in lowliness of mind, let each esteem others better than himself.

Let each of you look out not only for his own interests, but also for the interests of others.

Philippians 2:3,4

Here Paul wrote to the believers at Philippi concerning how to walk in the love of God and avoid the trap of walking in "natural" human love.

Be kindly affectionate to one another with brotherly love, in honor giving preference to one another.

Romans 12:10

Take a personal inventory of your life and see whether you are operating in human love or God's love. Look at:

- Your attitude to your spouse and children.

- Your attitude and words about other people.

- Your attitude toward your pastor and other leaders of your church.

- Your attitude toward yourself.

Ask yourself:

"Am I selfish?"

"Am I controlled by my emotions?"

"Am I always allowing my feelings to be affected?"

"Do I cry every time something is said about me?"

According to the Word of God, these types of reactions are childish. Paul wrote to the Corinthians to "put away childish things" and grow up spiritually. (1 Cor. 3:1-3.) That is advice for every Christian.

Mature – grow up in love – you *can* change. It will not happen overnight, but you will change if you begin with whatever problem is facing you now and continue to make choices to walk in love.

Do not try to justify your actions or deeds. Look at them as Jesus would. Do what Jesus would do! The longer you put off beginning the love walk, the longer it will take you to grow up in the Lord.

Not walking in love opens the door for envy and jealousy to steal your joy. You cannot be joyful and jealous at the same time. Envy is an enemy of love. Envy is dislike, hatred, and negative feelings.

Jealousy is being upset because someone else was blessed with something and you were not. To be *jealous* means seeing other people as competition to beat; to be suspicious or fearful of being displaced by another person.

Envy is wanting to get mad at someone or hurt them because they were blessed — or wanting to take it away from them!

Envy is jealousy "gone to seed," you might say, and many times, what begins as jealousy is allowed to eat away at a person's heart until it becomes envy. To be envious means that you have a grudging feeling of discontent towards another person's success, achievement, possessions, or position in life.

Envy is illegal desire that will cloud your mind, and as a Christian who wants to walk in victory, you cannot afford the luxury of strife, discord, or conflict in your life. (James 3:10-16.)

Envy breeds hatred and hostility, not only in you but against you. What you sow, you will reap. (Gal. 6:7.) Do not let Satan creep into your life and sow seeds of envy, jealousy, or bitterness. They will destroy you.

Envy breeds heaviness and kills your joy!

For where envy and self-seeking exist, confusion and every evil thing will be there.

James 3:16

Envy causes you to try and discredit the other person.

Learn what love really is and make choices to walk in it, if you truly want to be a mature Christian. I would say to you what John wrote in his first epistle:

My little children, let us not love in word or in tongue, but in deed and in truth.

1 John 3:18

Four Kinds of Love

The New Testament was written in Greek, and that language many times has more precise meanings for words than English. In English, *love* can mean many things, but in the original Greek, there are four words for love, and each word means a specific kind of love:

1. *Agape* is "divine love," something unsaved people do not have. This Greek word is used to express:

- God's love for the world. (John 3:16.)

- Christ's sacrificial love for His Church. (1 John 3:16.)

- The Holy Spirit's love flowing out of Christians to other people. (Rom. 5:5.)

Agape is the God-kind of love, which is the highest love of all. It is the direct opposite of conditional love, which is based on performance. This natural performance-based love says:

"I will love you *if* you do thus-and-so. When you stop pleasing me, or meeting my needs, I will stop loving you."

Divine love always says:

"I only want what is best for *you*. You are not an object to be bought and sold, used and discarded. You are not here to get "ripped off," taken advantage of, maneuvered, manipulated, or exploited."

Agape is a non-emotional love. It gives and gives without asking for anything in return.

Agape is God's love produced in the heart by the Holy Spirit — an unselfish love that motivates a person to deny himself for the sake of loving others.

Agape is the unconditional acceptance of other people and the active seeking of their highest good.

2. *Phileo* means "friendship," the affection we feel for people in friendly relationships. The affection of Saul's son Jonathan and David is a Bible example of this. (1 Sam. 18:1.)

3. *Storge* is the love we have for family members, such as Jacob had for his twelve sons. (Gen. 49:1.) Romans 12:10 says we are to treat Christians, our heavenly family, with "brotherly affection," which means with even more love and respect than we do our natural families.

4. *Eros* is the Greek word that denotes "sexual love." This is the entertainment world's definition of love.

Many marriages today are founded on *eros*, not *agape*, *phileo*, or *storge*. When something happens to the physical relationship, there is no other foundation. If the couple remains together, it is in an atmosphere of strife and contention. Many times, however, this relationship ends in divorce.

Sadly enough, both parties usually go on to repeat their mistakes, thinking that if they find the "right" person, they will be happy. What they need is to find the right kind of love and build a relationship on that.

No one can build a marriage, a family, or a true ministry on *storge*, *phileo*, or *eros*. True, lasting things can only be built on a true foundation: *agape*, God's love.

> **"But I say to you, love your enemies, bless those who curse you, do good to those who hate you, and pray for those who spitefully use you and persecute you,**
> **"That you may be sons of your Father in heaven; for He makes His sun rise on the evil and on the good, and sends rain on the just and on the unjust.**
> **"For if you love those who love you, what reward have you?"**
>
> **Matthew 5:44-46a**

I heard a story about a woman minister who was having problems with another minister in her hometown, a man who did not believe in women preachers. He persecuted her, even referring to her by name. She made a choice not to let this bother her and even prayed to the Lord to know what she could do for her persecutor.

She knew that his congregation was struggling, trying to pay for their church building. So she took up an offering and sent it to him. It was not long until the minister asked her to speak in his church. Because she stedfastly walked in love and *acted* in love, God moved on her behalf and turned the situation around.

If you have examined your life and want to change your definition of love, you may want to use this God-kind-of-love confession.

"I am born of love, and love is my nature; therefore:

I am patient and kind.

I do not let negative people or trying situations discourage me.

I choose to love; therefore, I am not envious or jealous of other people's blessings.

I am not arrogant.

I am not temperamental, easily upset, or moody.

I am not touchy or easily offended, but want to serve my fellow man and be a blessing to other people.

I do not think more highly of myself than I ought to (Rom. 12:3), but I do esteem myself as a child of God.

I am not rude and do not hold grudges against anyone.

I am not unforgiving or resentful.

Love is my nature. Therefore, I keep my tongue under control and my communication pure and undefiled.

I am born of love; therefore, I am a lover, not a fighter."

Key Thought: How you treat people shows what love means to you. Love is the proof that you genuinely have been born again. (1 John 3:14.)

3

LOVE IS A FIVE-LETTER WORD

Love has been perfected among us. . . that we may have boldness in the day of judgment; because as He is, so are we in this world.

1 John 4:17

Many of God's people today are not lacking in the knowledge of God's Word, neither are they lacking in their confessions of faith, nor in their believing of God's Word. But they *are* falling short and missing victory by not walking in the love of God.

What the Bible says about love needs to be absorbed into our spirits and allowed to renew our minds. As this mind-renewing process takes place, it will begin to affect our lifestyles and our relationships. Walking in love is not an instant, overnight accomplishment. It is a progressive transformation brought about by choices and actions after we understand what real love is like.

In English, *love* has four letters, but real love as defined in the Bible and expressed in the original Greek is *agape*, so true love is a five-letter word.

Polly Wigglesworth

Love is unselfish and always puts other people first. The late Smith Wigglesworth, noted British evangelist, was won to the Lord by the unselfish and loving actions of his wife, Polly. No matter how harshly he acted toward her, she always responded in love.

Wigglesworth often related something that happened while he was in a backslidden condition. He came to resent his wife's going to church three times a week. He thought that was too much, although she did not neglect him or their children.

So, knowing that the Bible says the man is "head of the house," he put his foot down and forbade her to go to church any more. However, his wife very firmly told him that, yes, he was her husband and head of the house, *but* he was not the Lord Jesus. She had to obey the Lord, who said to go to church – so she kept on going to church.

Finally, Wigglesworth told his wife that the next time she went, he would lock her out. And he did. She came home, knocked on the door, and he would not let her in. The night was a very cold one, and she spent it huddled up outside against the door. When he opened the door the next morning, she almost fell into the kitchen, chilled and stiff.

Yet she jumped up, smiling, and said, "Dear, what would you like for breakfast?"

He related this story many times during his ministry. Wigglesworth always said that if it had not been for Polly's loving attitude, he would not have made it. And the Church would have lost the fruits of a man who became a very great apostle of faith, mightily used by God.

Walking in love cannot be done out of your feelings. I cannot overemphasize this. Love is a decision of faith to love people even when they are difficult and unlovely. Sometimes the greatest tests of love are those between husband and wife, as Wigglesworth's story shows.

A Husband Sold Out to Love

In a recent article in *Ministries Today*, evangelist Jack Taylor shared another true story that is a prime example of a husband who is as sold out to walking in the true love of God as Polly Wigglesworth was.[1]

Taylor wrote of a man who was president of a college and seminary with a multimillion-dollar budget, a large faculty, and a program of study with many facets that reached around the world. In his mid-50s, his wife developed Alzheimer's disease.

Over a period of years, her condition declined. The college's board of trustees arranged for a companion to stay with her, but she only felt secure when her husband was there. She would slip off and follow him to the office, often arriving there with her feet blistered and bloody.

Without any long deliberation at all, the husband retired from his position and is spending the rest of his life looking after his wife. He says it is only fair, seeing that she had spent about forty years looking after him.

He says that if he must take care of her for the next forty years, he would not be out of debt to her. He considers this small repayment for the devotion and care with which she had made it possible for him to accomplish his work for God.

"I don't *have* to care for her," he says, "I *get to.*"

I wonder how many husbands or wives in the Church today would be able to "go and do likewise"?

Marriage is the first place, the first relationship where God wants to work out the hindrances to walking in love that exist in our lives. If you can truly talk and act in love within your home and marriage, you will have no problem with outsiders.

I heard a minister say one time, "If the Gospel doesn't work in your home, then don't export it."

And that is very good advice!

---

[1]Taylor, Jack. "The Greatest Preacher," *Ministries Today* (Lake Mary, Florida), Vol. 11, No. 6, November/December, 1993, pp. 36,37.

Understanding the God-Kind of Love

Here are some more things the Bible says about love, which I believe will help you better understand what real love truly is like.

- Love is a commandment. (John 13:34.)

- Love is shed abroad in our hearts by the Holy Spirit. (Rom. 5:5.)

- Love is the fulfilling of the law. (Rom. 13:10.)

- Love is the catalyst that gives meaning to speaking in tongues, to prophesying, to understanding God and His ways, to charitable works, and to self-sacrifice. (1 Cor. 13:1-3.)

- Love is kind. (1 Cor. 13:4.)

- Love is greater than faith. (1 Cor. 13:13.)

- Love is greater than hope. (1 Cor. 13:13.)

- Love is the bond of perfectness. (Col. 3:14.)

- Love is living according to God's commandments. (2 John 6.)

- Love is not envious, puffed up, or easily provoked. (1 Cor. 13: 4,5.)

- Love is a force, a fruit, an influence. (Gal. 5:22,23.)

- Love is a spirit, an attribute, and a product of the nature of God and the Spirit of God who lives within you. (1 John 4:7,8.)

- Love is a spiritual substance in your reborn spirit. When you release love out of your heart, it influences, touches, and changes people around you. (1 John 4:11,12.)

- Love means consistently treating other people the way you would like them to treat you — with respect, courtesy, and consideration. (1 John 4:20.)

- Love is a good listener and tolerant of others' differences. (John 15:12,13.)

We should make sure that the world sees Jesus *in* us before we try to tell them *about* Jesus.

If the world cannot see love in us, why should they want what we have? It was Gandhi who made the strong statement: "The whole world would be Christian, if it wasn't for the Christians!"

We will never reach the unsaved for Jesus by trying to convince their minds that our beliefs are better than anyone else's.

We will only reach them by showing them we *have* something better than every other belief: *love*. God's love in us and flowing through us will have an impact upon those who hear us more than anything else.

Love's Definition

First Corinthians 13 is God's definition of love and expresses His attitude toward us as well as the attitudes He wants us to have toward one another.

> **Though I speak with the tongues of men and of angels, but have not love** (*agape*)**, I have become as sounding brass** ("a noisy gong") **or a clanging cymbal.**
>
> **And though I have the gift of prophecy, and understand all mysteries and all knowledge, and though I have all faith so that I could remove mountains but have not love, I am nothing.** ("I am a useless nobody!")
>
> **And though I bestow all my goods to feed the poor, and though I give my body to be burned, but have not love, it profits me nothing.** ("I achieve nothing.")
>
> **Love suffers long and is kind; love does not envy; love does not parade itself, is not puffed up;**
>
> **Does not behave rudely, does not seek its own, is not provoked, thinks no evil;**
>
> **Does not rejoice in iniquity, but rejoices in the truth;**
>
> **Bears all things, believes all things, hopes all things, endures all things.**
>
> **Love never fails. . . .**
>
> **And now abide faith, hope, love, these three; but the greatest of these is love.**
>
> **1 Corinthians 13:1-8,13**

Verse four says that *love:*

— does not envy and never boils with jealousy.

— makes no parade of its own virtues and is not proud.

— puts on no airs, neither does it cherish inflated ideas of its own importance.

— does not brag or have an inflated ego.

— penetrates the whole nature, making tender everything that was hard.

Verse five really says that *love:*

— has good manners and is never rude.

— does not demand its own way or pursue its own selfish desires.

— is never irritable or resentful.

— is not touchy or quick to take offense.

Verses six, seven, and eight say that *love:*

— is never glad about injustice.

— takes no pleasure in unrighteousness.

— rejoices at the victory of truth.

— has unquenchable faith and bears up under anything that comes.

— knows no limit to its endurance and no end to its trust.

— can outlast anything and will always succeed.

Love is always ready to believe the best of every person.

Love never fails to love, Paul wrote.

Pretty Teeth

I heard a story about a man who had such a reputation for being loving and kind that he would never say anything bad or critical about anyone. Then one day the meanest man in town died, and everyone waited for this kind-hearted man to come to the funeral. They all wondered what in the world he would do. Surely this time, he would have to break his principle. There simply *was not anything* good to be said about the dead man!

But when the man stopped in front of the casket to view the deceased, he looked for some minutes, and then said, "Well, he certainly had pretty teeth." He was simply determined to find something good to say about the person and would not say anything critical.

Key Thought: Love is not only a choice but an action, a constraining force that enables us to talk right, act right, and live right.

4

FAITH WORKS BY LOVE

For in Christ Jesus neither circumcision nor uncircumcision avails anything, but faith working through love.

Galatians 5:6

Jesus always walked in love and compassion, healing the sick and delivering those bound by Satan. Several times in the Gospels, we read that Jesus "was moved with compassion" for those in need. The miracle multiplication of the loaves and fishes began with Jesus being filled with compassion for the multitude who were so hungry for spiritual food that they had gone three days without food for their bodies. (Matt. 15:32.)

Jesus loved those people and immediately put His faith into action. Healing was always a result. As a matter of fact, the foundation for the healing ministry of Jesus — and for anyone since Jesus — is the love of God. Anyone filled with the love of God will "go about doing good."

. . . God anointed Jesus of Nazareth with the Holy Spirit and with power, who went about doing good and healing all who were oppressed by the devil, for God was with Him.

Acts 10:38

Compassion is God's love in action.

Compassion is much more than human sympathy, which many times is based on emotion or sentimentality, not genuine compassion flowing out of love.

And when Jesus went out He saw a great multitude; and He was moved with compassion for them, and healed their sick.

Matthew 14:14

45

Compassion, or God's love in operation, is the reason for the gifts of the Spirit being manifested through God's people to meet the needs of others.

The Power of God's Love

The anointing, power, and gifts of the Holy Spirit are made available to us to minister to people in need, not to build the reputation of those called to five-fold offices. Some ministers want to have a healing ministry simply to get a crowd of people to attend their meetings. There are even some whose motives in getting a crippled person to walk out of a wheelchair is to have photographs to run on the front page of their newsletters.

Of course, I believe the majority of ministers want to have the right motives and usually do. In our own services, the power of God is in strong demonstration simply because we allow the love of God and the compassion of Jesus to flow as the foundation for the gifts of the Spirit. The purpose of the anointing is always to minister to the needs of people.

> "The Spirit of the Lord is upon Me,
> Because He has anointed Me to preach
>   the gospel to the poor.
> He has sent Me to heal the brokenhearted,
> To preach deliverance to the captives
> And recovery of sight to the blind,
> To set at liberty those who are oppressed,
> To preach the acceptable year of the Lord."
>
> Luke 4:18,19

During a series of revival services in Michigan, a 12-year-old girl, totally blind in her right eye, was healed instantly of a detached-retina condition. In the same week of meetings, a lady walked out of a wheelchair, and another was healed of cystic fibrosis. These were just a few of the many outstanding healings and miracles that happened during the revival.

One of the most powerful healings that took place when the love of God was so strong in a service occurred several years ago in Johannesburg, South Africa.

A mother brought her teenage daughter up to the altar for prayer. The girl had broken her coccyx that week playing sports at school, and she was in agonizing pain.

As I laid hands on her, the power of the Holy Spirit moved upon me with great compassion.

Like surges of electricity, the healing virtue of God totally and instantly healed this terrible injury. The teenager immediately could touch her toes without pain.

Jesus Never Changes

Jesus is the same yesterday, today, and forever. (Heb. 13:8.)

If we allow His love to flow through us, His miracle power will minister to the sick and the afflicted today just as it did when He walked on earth.

Every place my wife and I minister, we see the power of God operating. Multitudes of healings have taken place. These have involved every kind of condition:

Asthma, deafness, arthritis, all types of cancer, heart problems, lupus, neck and back injuries, cataracts, nerve and blood disorders, club feet, tumors and growths, Hodgkins and Parkinson's diseases, cystic fibrosis, even teeth problems, as well as many others.

Why do these things happen in our meetings?

It is not because we are better than other ministries, or because we have any "edge" on others in operating in the gifts of the Spirit. We believe these things happen for one reason:

The love of God releases the power of God.

And we truly feel the love of God for those standing before us in need of healing and deliverance.

The Holy Spirit uses us as available vessels for the love of God to flow through. We sometimes look at the hurting people in front of us – bound with sicknesses and diseases because of the devil – and feel an overwhelming compassion that is almost more than we can contain.

If our motives were not right, and if we had not chosen in our hearts to care about the people, I do not believe this would happen. The love of God flowing through anyone's services builds faith.

Let Love Be Your Foundation

"Whoever comes to Me, and hears My sayings and does them, I will show you whom he is like:

"He is like a man building a house, who dug deep and laid the foundation on the rock. And when the flood arose, the stream beat vehemently against that house, and could not shake it, for it was founded on the rock.

"But he who heard and did nothing is like a man who built a house on the earth without a foundation, against which the stream beat vehemently; and immediately it fell. And the ruin of that house was great."

Luke 6:47-49

The single biggest reason for faith not working and prayers going unanswered is lack of walking the love walk.

Faith is extremely important in the Christian life. We receive everything from God by faith. However, the Word of God tells us very plainly that faith *works* by love.

A building is only as good or as strong as its foundation.

Many Christians have the mistaken idea that by knowing all the right scriptures and all the right spiritual "formulas," they can get any prayer answered. They are attempting to erect a "faith building" without any foundation or building on the "sand," the wrong foundation.

These people have what I call "an ostrich mentality." They ignore the trials, tests, and problems of life, thinking in error that Christians do not have to experience these things.

We experience the same things mankind always has experienced since the Garden of Eden. The difference is that we do not have to let those things get the best of us.

Many times people are defeated by trials, tests, and problems because their faith is based on a presumptuous or a false idea of God, not on the Word of God.

Nowhere in the Bible did God "promise us a rose garden" here on earth. What He *did* do was promise us the way of escape and victory over temptations. (1 Cor. 10:13.) In Christ, we have the ability to overcome the day-to-day situations and negative circumstances that come against us, because greater is He who is in us than anything that faces us in the world. (1 John 4:4.)

The New Testament is filled with victory principles to enable us to effectively deal with this world. A vital key God gave us to enable us to live happy, successful, and prosperous lives on earth is "walking in love."

But above all these things put on love, which is the bond of perfection.

Colossians 3:14

Faith works by love, the Bible says, but what does that really mean?

How Does Faith Work?

The word *work* means "to cause to function" or "to bring about effects." That means essentially that faith without love will not produce results but will be ineffective. James wrote that **faith without works is dead** (James 2:20,26).

In other words, faith that is not expressed with corresponding *action* is not faith.

If you are walking in love, you will have corresponding actions — and love will cause faith to bring results.

An overwhelming compassion (God's love in action) that flows through you toward someone else will culminate in some kind of action toward that person. Your faith in God's desire to help and in His ability to help has found a vehicle through which it can move. That vehicle is *love*.

Paul wrote in 1 Corinthians 13:13 that of the three greatest attributes of the Christian life — faith, hope, and love — love is the greatest! That is because love is the ultimate royal law underlying God's creation and redemption of man.

Without love, there is no hope. (Rom. 5:5.)

Without hope, you will never get to the point where faith can be exercised. (Heb. 11:1.)

Without faith, you will receive nothing from God. (Heb. 11:6.)

The steps toward receiving everything God has for you are these:

1. Love God first and your neighbor as yourself.

2. Then you can have hope that the things you desire will become a reality, because *love* never fails.

3. The faith you have in God and His Word will work to accomplish its purpose.

Faith will *not* work:

— in an unforgiving heart.

— if you are walking in strife, discord, or living in disharmony.

— if your heart is filled with jealousy and envy or other ill feelings toward others.

Faith *will* work:

— as you walk in love, agreement and harmony.

Again I tell you, if two of you on earth agree (harmonize together, make a symphony together) about whatever

[anything and everything] they may ask, it will come to pass and be done for them by My Father in heaven.

For wherever two or three are gathered (drawn together as My followers) in (into) My name, there I AM in the midst of them.

Matthew 18:19,20 AMP

Developing a Servant's Heart

Your faith will start working for you as you truly develop a servant's heart toward others.

It is not possible to be a true servant without a loving heart or without walking in love. And, to be a good leader, one must first be a good servant.

". . . Whoever desires to become great among you, let him be your servant.

"And whoever desires to be first among you, let him be your slave —

"Just as the Son of Man did not come to be served, but to serve, and to give His life a ransom for many."

Matthew 20:26-28

"But he who is greatest among you shall be your servant.

"And whoever exalts himself will be abased, and he who humbles himself will be exalted."

Matthew 23:11,12

Many Christians would not be living victorious spiritual lives today without the "faith message." However, I have seen a lot of people who have taken that message and are living "lopsided" (unbalanced) spiritual lives.

If we are victorious, successful, and prosperous, yet at the same time, full of ego, arrogance, and pride, how are we any different from the world?

Sooner or later, faith that does not work by love will fail because it is not Biblically based. You can tell what foundation a person's faith is on by listening to them talk.

Do they restore a child of God who has fallen into sin?

Or, do they gossip about, criticize, and exude self-righteousness toward that person? Too many ministers think that God has appointed them as the sheriff in the Church.

Paul wrote the church at Galatia to restore someone "overtaken in any trespass." He pointed out that they also could be tempted into sin, so they should have a "spirit of gentleness" toward such a person. (Gal. 6:1.)

In the Body of Christ, we are not called to be *exposers*, but *restorers*.

The only time exposing someone's sin is scriptural is when someone refuses to repent and be restored but rather continues in sin and rebellion, making a mockery of the blood of Jesus.

Peter wrote, as did King Solomon in Proverbs 10:12:

And above all things have fervent love for one another, for "love will cover a multitude of sins."

1 Peter 4:8

Getting Results When You Pray

Not one of us can change our pasts – the mistakes, the failures, sins, and all of the negative experiences. All we *can* do is receive the cleansing blood of Christ to wipe the slate clean and redeem us from the past. However, through God's Word, we *can* change the present and shape the future.

With the help of the Holy Spirit, we can speak, walk, and act differently than we did in the past.

Many times, the reason prayers are not answered lies primarily with the one who is praying! It certainly is not God who fails to answer. If your prayers are not answered:

• *Check yourself on the basis of God's Word.*

Are you praying according to His will?

Are your prayers based on Scripture?

• *Check your motives.*

Are you asking for things to lavish on your own "lusts" because of a covetous heart?

• *Check your "love life."*

Are you operating in a cold, judgmental attitude to others?

Are you holding onto grudges and bitterness at others?

• *Check your faith.*

Are you praying in faith?

Are you walking in faith, or are you full of doubt and unbelief?

Faith works the same in any area of the Christian walk, from salvation to divine health and prosperity to right-standing with God. To develop your faith in God's love or in anything else from God, you must first learn what the Word says about it. (Rom. 10:17.)

You should never base your faith on how you *feel* about God's love. If you were brought up in an unhappy home where your earthly father neglected or abused you, then more than likely, you will "feel" that your heavenly Father also does not love you. However, *the Bible says over and over that He does!* Child of God, have faith in God's love for you.

Walk by *faith*, and not by *sight*. (2 Cor. 5:7.)

Choose to believe what the Word says, not what your feelings say. If you have a problem believing in God's love for you, read the book of 1 John over and over on a regular basis. Also, get a concordance and look up all of the references to God's love.

Meditate on those scriptures. Meditation develops the capacity for faith. Meditation means to think the thoughts of God – to dwell upon His promises. As you meditate in God's Word and your faith capacity begins to grow, you will begin to truly believe in God's love for you and for all mankind.

God so loved *the world* that He sent Jesus to die for every person ever born. However, that tremendous act of love on God's part will avail nothing for a person who does not *receive* His love by faith.

There are several ways to perfect the love of God in your life:

First of all, obey the Word of God by putting every aspect of your life under the lordship of Jesus Christ.

Secondly, believe the love God has for you, and renew your mind with love scriptures.

Thirdly, practice His love on others through decisions and actions — go out of your way to be a blessing to people. As you do this, the foundation of your faith will become firm and unshakable, and your life will align with God's perfect will and purpose. You will not succeed every time when you first start out on the love walk, of course. This walk is a progressive, day-by-day journey.

The book of Romans tells us that the ultimate goal of the Christian life is for us to be conformed to the image of Jesus (Rom. 8:29), and we certainly do not arrive there overnight.

As we aim to move towards that goal, there are many opportunities for mistakes and failures.

If you fail, simply repent, and begin again.

You can become "love-of-God conscious" through the confession of your mouth and by your actions.

The things that came to pass in your past and that are coming to pass in your present are the result of what is in your heart: fear or faith, hatred and bitterness or love, anxiety or peace? (Proverbs 4:23.)

What has been in *your* heart?

There is no shortcut to walking in love. You must take the time to fill your heart with God's Word, and you must practice the Word.

Does *your* heart need changing?

What is your response to the teaching in this chapter?

Perhaps it is time you make some adjustments in your life. Here are some practical steps to help you:

1. Be honest with yourself. Pinpoint any problem in your life.

2. Get rid of it by confessing it as sin, releasing it, applying 1 John 1:9, and being cleansed by the blood of Christ. Repentance is the pathway to victory.

3. Rely on the Holy Spirit to help you overcome the problem areas in your life. You cannot deal with wrong attitudes by yourself.

4. Realize that every person is equally valuable and precious to God — including you but also not excluding anyone, no matter what you may think of certain people.

5. Make a habit of going out of your way to be a blessing to people around you. Practice being a doer of God's Word by daily sowing seeds of love through your words and actions. Remember the Bible law of sowing and reaping applies in the love walk just as much as finances.

Key Thought: We are *faith* children of a *faith* God.

We are *love* children of a *love* God.

THE CHALLENGE OF LOVE: FORGIVENESS

> Therefore I say unto you: whatever things you ask when you pray, believe that you receive them, and you will have them.
>
> And whenever you stand praying, if you have anything against anyone, forgive him, that your Father in heaven may also forgive you your trespasses.
>
> But if you do not forgive, neither will your Father in heaven forgive your trespasses.
>
> **Mark 11:24-26**

We get excited about Mark 11:23,24, but sometimes we forget about the following two verses. Jesus said that our prayers being answered, even with "faith to move mountains" (Matt. 17:20) depends on not having unforgiveness in our hearts.

Paul wrote:

> . . . And though I have all faith, so that I could remove mountains, but have not love, I am nothing.
>
> **1 Corinthians 13:2**

Learning to forgive is a vital step in a Christian's spiritual growth. You might say *forgiveness* is the ultimate challenge to walking in love.

Without forgiveness, there is no love.

Without forgiveness, God cannot forgive you. (Mark 11:25,26.)

When Jesus said that if we do not forgive others, our Father in Heaven will not forgive us, He was talking to believers — not sinners. It is a grave mistake for Christians to think that it is all right for them not to forgive others, no matter how serious the offense was.

Many people miss God by thinking *they* have a right to hold grudges. After all, they were the injured parties!

Kenneth Hagin tells of a conversation his wife once overheard during a church service. Two women were sitting behind her talking about a third woman who had just come into the church.

Apparently, the newcomer had stolen a boyfriend from one of the women at some time in the past. The "injured party" said something like this:

"Look at her coming into church as if she were a good Christian woman, and her not even saved!"

The other woman said, "Why, how do you know she's not saved? I always thought she was."

And the first woman said, "No, she's not! I won't forgive her, and if I don't forgive her, God won't!"

That woman had it completely backwards, of course. If she did not forgive the woman who stole her boyfriend, then *she* was the one God could not forgive.

What a tragic misunderstanding!

Yet many Christians seem to feel the same way, or they think someone who offends them is supposed to come to them first and ask for forgiveness. They say things like this:

"I didn't do anything to him. He is the one who treated me badly. Let him come to me, and I will forgive him."

That is not what the Bible says.

Other people stumble over forgiving someone more than once. Jesus told Peter to forgive "seventy times seven" (four hundred and ninety times)! He did not mean in a day, nor even in a year.

What Jesus was saying is that we must have an unlimited capacity to forgive, because God has shown His unlimited capacity to forgive us. (Matt. 18:21,22.)

Some people may say, "Well, I have forgiven So-and-so, but I'm not going to forget!"

People who say that have never really forgiven. When God forgives our sins, He puts them as far away from Him "as the east is from the west" (Ps. 103:12) and remembers them against us no more. That is what He wants us to do with those who have offended us and hurt us.

Someone has said that forgiveness should be like cancelling a note against someone who owes you something. The note should be torn in two and burned, so that it can never place anyone in debt again.

When you forgive someone, you are saying, "You don't owe me anything. I forgive and release that debt I was holding against you, because my Father in Heaven has forgiven me a much greater one."

The Chains of Unforgiveness

People need to realize that they are not hurting the ones who hurt them by refusing to forgive them. They are only hurting themselves. Perhaps that person does not care, or does not know he has offended.

Unforgiveness ties the offense to you, so that you drag it around with you the rest of your life. Unless you allow Jesus to cut the chains of unforgiveness away by forgiving the offense, you will never be free from it.

If we could see them in the spiritual realm, many Christians might look like Marley in Charles Dickens' classic story, *The Christmas Carol*, dragging around heavy boxes and bales of unforgiveness!

The weight of bitterness and resentment that results from unforgiveness can have an effect on your physical well-being. A heart of unforgiveness can be reflected in arthritis or other diseases that stiffen and twist the physical body. The Bible calls this crippling condition a "spirit of infirmity." (Luke 13:11.)

Not all such diseases are caused by unforgiveness, but it can certainly be a contributing cause. I have seen dramatic instant healings in people who finally were willing to forgive others for offenses.

Bitterness is like an unhealed and festering sore that continually boils over with the poison of unforgiveness. It shows in your voice and your conversation, as well as possibly affecting your body.

> **A sound heart is life to the body,**
> **But envy is rottenness to the bones.**
>
> **Proverbs 14:30**

> **The spirit of a man will sustain him**
> **in sickness,**
> **But who can bear a broken spirit?**
>
> **Proverbs 18:14**

Do you know what happens when you begin to hold grudges?

It is the same thing spiritually that happens to the arteries around your heart in the natural when too much fat is taken into the body. Fat collects around the edges of the arteries and restricts the flow of blood. Once it begins, it builds up and builds up until the artery is so clogged that *no* blood can get through.

Unforgiveness builds up the same way.

Unforgiveness begins collecting in the channel where the Spirit flows. If we are not careful, it will clog that channel until nothing from the Holy Spirit is flowing at all. Every Christian needs to live free from unforgiveness so his spiritual arteries are clear and without any kind of blockage.

The High Cost of Unforgiveness

A middle-aged Christian woman had played the piano every week at her church for years. But one day a new pastor came to the church and began to make all kinds of changes. One of these was to ask this woman to play only one week a month.

His idea was to increase the number of musicians on the worship team, to get other people involved. But the pianist was so offended that she soon resigned from her position saying she felt "God was leading her" to take a rest.

Over the process of time, she allowed the grudge at the pastor to take root inside her. The feelings of unforgiveness and resentment began to take root, and her physical health became affected. In the following year, bitterness caused severe arthritis to afflict her body, and after eighteen months, her hands and fingers were twisted in agonizing pain. She could no longer play the piano even if she had wanted to.

She attended church a number of times to receive prayer for healing, but could not get healed. Then she began to get in the healing line of every evangelist who came through her city, but nothing happened. She contacted ministries on Christian television and radio programs, requesting prayer, but to no avail. Her condition only grew worse.

One Sunday morning some months later, a visiting evangelist in her local church had a "word of knowledge" that her condition was related to unforgiveness in her heart.

Immediately this lady was convicted, realizing how wrong she had been to harbor resentment at her pastor. Before any prayer was offered up, she apologized publicly to the pastor, repented, and released all of the pent-up bitterness from her heart.

The moment she did that and without prayer or laying on of hands, her hands and fingers straightened out supernaturally by the power of God. The arthritis and pain totally left her.

Recently, while ministering in a New Orleans church, I shared this story. About thirty people came forward for prayer to release unforgiveness from their hearts. One of them was a Creole lady who also had crippling arthritis in her hands. Again, without prayer for healing, she was set free instantly as soon as she released unforgiveness.

It has been my experience in many places where I have ministered that there is a connection between unforgiveness and crippling diseases such as arthritis. No matter who has wronged you, let it go for your own good.

Perhaps you were abused as a child, even sexually molested.

Perhaps you were cheated in a business deal or had thousands of dollars stolen from you.

Perhaps people have lied and gossiped about you.

Maybe you went through a painful marriage break-up.

Whatever has happened to you, let go of it before it destroys you! Make a decision to get free from unforgiveness, anger, and bitterness. Unforgiveness is a luxury no Christian can afford. It costs too much in spiritual and physical wages.

Unforgiveness Hinders the Church

One of the biggest problems in the Church today is unforgiveness. It not only hinders spiritual growth in individuals; it hinders God's work in general.

• *Unforgiveness causes problems in congregations.*

When people sit week after week holding grudges against one another, the Holy Spirit cannot move freely in that place. Their attitudes "clog up" the spiritual body, hindering and at times even halting the flow of the Holy Spirit. Many people sit in church dwelling on their grievances and playing into the devil's hands.

• *Unforgiveness hinders praise and worship.*

How can you praise God with bitterness in your heart? It is not possible.

• *Unforgiveness hinders unity.*

Holding grudges and making judgments against those who do not believe exactly as you do hinders unity in the Body of Christ.

There are a number of things in the Bible (for example end-time prophecy and the Book of Revelation) that are subject to different interpretations. Please do not fight over things in the Bible or in Christianity that have different possible interpretations. We can disagree, but let's do it in love and not become disagreeable.

Unity is based on *relationship*. We already are united with everyone who has been born again into God's family, but so often, we do not walk in "family love." Many Christians are going to be surprised at the people they will find in Heaven.

Unity is not based on agreement of doctrines. The only prerequisite for spending eternity in Heaven is being born again by personal faith in the blood of the Lord Jesus Christ.

Unity in the Body is not based on believing in healing, or prosperity, or even the baptism of the Holy Spirit. It is not based on everyone believing the same prophetic scenario for endtimes. In Heaven, many Christians will fellowship with people whom they ignored on earth because they did not believe the same things. When God's people flow together in love and unity, that is the place where the full blessing of God rests.

> **Behold, how good and how pleasant it is**
> **For brethren to dwell together in unity!**
> **It is like the precious oil upon the head,**
> **Running down on the beard,**
> **The beard of Aaron.**
> **Running down on the edge of his garments.**
> **It is like the dew of Hermon,**
> **Descending upon the mountains of Zion;**
> **For there the Lord commanded the blessing —**
> **Life forevermore.**
>
> **Psalm 133:1-3**

Dwelling upon negative comments or critical words spoken about you by others will hinder you from walking in love and unity.

Never permit anything said about you to remain in your memory. If you think on negative things long enough, they will begin to affect you. Negative words are like "seeds" planted in your mind, and they will spring up into a whole crop of weeds if you let them take root and grow.

> **For the rest, brethren, whatever is true, whatever is worthy of reverence and is honorable and seemly, whatever is just, whatever is pure, whatever is lovely and lovable, whatever is kind and winsome and gracious, if there is any virtue and excellence, if there is anything worthy of praise, think on and weigh and take account of these things — fix your minds on them.**
>
> **Philippians 4:8 AMP**

Evangelist Kenneth Copeland says the Lord told him not to read anything written about himself – good or bad. That is sound advice!

Release From Unforgiveness

If your prayers are not being answered, the first thing to check is whether love is undergirding your faith. Or is there someone against whom you are holding a grudge? If you harbor unforgiveness long enough, you will begin to act on it and actively sin against someone else.

The person who wronged you has to answer to God. You only have to answer to God for yourself. The only thing you can do for them is to forgive them, pray for them, and continue to walk in love.

> **Be gentle and forbearing with one another and, if one has a difference (a grievance or complaint) against another, readily pardoning each other; even as the Lord has freely forgiven you, so must you also [forgive].**
>
> **Colossians 3:13 AMP**

You may think you are in control when you refuse to forgive; however, that is not true. The person who wronged you is controlling *you* through your unforgiveness. You will never be free of that incident if *you* do not let it go. Do not allow unforgiveness to be a blockage in your life today. (Mark 11:25,26.)

If you are carrying a load of bitterness, anger, and unforgiveness inside, pray this prayer right now and get free from it:

"Lord Jesus, I thank You for shedding Your blood at the cross and dying for me in order that I may receive the forgiveness of all of my sins.

Today, with the help of the Holy Spirit, I make the decision to forgive everyone who has ever hurt me in any way. Now I release all unforgiveness, resentment, and bitterness out of my heart in Jesus' name.

Thank you, Lord, that because You have forgiven me much, I can forgive others. I thank You that because I have forgiven others, You will forgive me for the sin of unforgiveness. I choose to walk in love and forgiveness and give the devil no place in my life, in Jesus' name! Amen"

Key Thought: Unforgiveness hurts you, not the other person.

CONCLUSION: PRACTICAL KEYS TO IMPROVING YOUR LOVE LIFE

> There is no fear in love; but perfect love casts out fear, because fear involves torment. But he who fears has not been made perfect in love.
>
> **1 John 4:18**

Every born-again believer *can* walk in love, if he or she chooses to make that decision. We have seen that part of our inheritance as children of God is His nature given to us. We are born of God, and love *is* God. (2 Pet. 1:4; 1 John 4:7,8.)

Here are some insights that we have learned in this book:

• Walking in love is the personal responsibility of each Christian — a commandment from Jesus, not an option.

• Walking in love is not based on feelings or emotions, but is a quality decision based on God's Word.

• Walking in love eliminates all fear from your life.

• Walking in love requires that you guard your tongue and avoid corrupt communication.

• Walking in love involves living free from unforgiveness and bitterness, regardless of how people have hurt you.

• Walking in love is the foundation for faith to truly work.

• Walking in love is not an instant, overnight change, but a progressive spiritual development.

Be kindly affectionate to one another with brotherly love, in honor giving preference to one another.

Romans 12:10

If you have made a decision to truly begin walking in love, here are seven keys that will improve your "love life":

1. Spend time in prayer and let the Holy Spirit help you uproot and remove any bitterness, resentment, or hurts.

2. Read, meditate, and confess 1 Corinthians 13:4-8 daily until it becomes a part of your life. Confess these scriptures and others on love over your life twice a day for the next seven days.

3. Pray daily for someone you dislike or find it difficult to get along with. Pray with your understanding and pray in the Spirit. (Rom. 8:26,27.)

4. Refuse to entertain any negative thoughts about anyone for the next seven days.

5. Refuse to say or repeat anything negative about anyone for the next seven days.

6. Really listen to people with love and concern for the next seven days, especially people who usually bore you.

7. Tell someone, "I love you," each day for the next seven days, someone in addition to family members and close friends.

When the seven days are up, begin all over again. What looks impossible in the beginning will gradually become an established part of your life.

Key Scriptures for Improving Your Love Life

In addition to the scriptures on love given as references or printed out in this book, here are some others on which to meditate.

Above all things have intense and unfailing love for one another, for love covers a multitude of sins [forgives and disregards the offenses of others].

1 Peter 4:8 AMP

You shall not take vengeance, nor bear any grudge against the children of your people, but you shall love your neighbor as yourself: I am the Lord.

Leviticus 19:18

For I am persuaded that neither death nor life, nor angels nor principalities nor powers, nor things present nor things to come,

Nor height nor depth, nor any other created thing, shall be able to separate us from the love of God which is in Christ Jesus our Lord.

Romans 8:38,39

Love does no wrong to one's neighbor [it never hurts anybody]. Therefore love meets all the requirements and is the fulfilling of the Law.

Romans 13:10 AMP

. . . Knowledge puffs up, but love edifies.

1 Corinthians 8:1

And let us consider one another in order to stir up love and good works.

Hebrews 10:24

Therefore, as the elect of God, holy and beloved, put on tender mercies, kindness, humbleness of mind, meekness, longsuffering;

Bearing with one another, and forgiving one another, if anyone has a complaint against another; even as Christ forgave you, so you also must do.

But above all these things put on love, which is the bond of perfection.

Colossians 3:12-14

But whoever keeps His word, truly the love of God is perfected in him. By this we know that we are in Him.

1 John 2:5

By this we know love, because He laid down His life for us. And we also ought to lay down our lives for the brethren.

1 John 3:16

And what this love consists in is this, that we live and walk in accordance with and guided by His commandments — His orders, ordinances, precepts, teaching. This is the commandment, as you have heard from the beginning, that you continue to walk in love — guided by it and following it.

2 John 6 AMP

We know that we have passed from death to life, because we love the brethren. He who does not love his brother abides in death.

1 John 3:14

A Love Declaration

The following is a love declaration based on 1 Corinthians 13 that I pray will also help you change the mind-set that has hindered the love of God from flowing in your life.

- I am born of God, so God's love is in me.

- I choose to walk in love and stay in love, because love is my nature as a born-again Christian.

- I am patient, kind, and longsuffering, not easily upset.

- I am not envious or jealous of other people's blessings.

- I am not arrogant or puffed up and do not brag or boast, nor do I exalt myself.

- I walk in love; therefore, I do not hold grudges against anyone. Consequently, I am not unforgiving or resentful.

- I am not rude, but have the good manners that come from walking in love.

- I walk in love, so I am not selfish nor self-seeking but always put other people first.

- I am not touchy, moody, or temperamental.

- I believe and look for the best in every person.

- I walk in love, so I keep my tongue under control being careful not to criticize or "bad-mouth" anyone. Nor do I spread rumors and gossip.

- I walk in love, so I do not argue or give people a piece of my mind. In fact, I cover up the faults and mistakes of other people.

- I walk in love, so I am a blessing to people around me. I think only good things about them and myself, and I speak only good things about everyone. If I cannot say something good, then I do not say anything at all.

- Daily, I am increasing and developing in the God-kind of love.

Let all that you do be done with love.

1 Corinthians 16:14

LET ME HEAR FROM YOU

I pray and believe that you have been encouraged and strengthened by the message of this book and it has caused you to grow spiritually. It always means a great deal to me to hear testimonies about how our teaching ministry is changing people's lives. So if you have been blessed and helped through this ministry, please take time today to write me and share your words of encouragement.

Also, when you write please pray about supporting this ministry financially so we can touch many more lives with the power of the Gospel.

If you feel that God is leading you to be involved in supporting this ministry, please fill out the following and along with your offering mail it to our address.

☐ Yes! I want to support your ministry with my monthly gift of $_____.

☐ Enclosed is my one-time gift of $_____.

☐ I am enclosing a special missions offering for the overseas outreaches of Norman Robertson Ministries $_____.

Thank you for your financial support, and I know that the seeds you have sown into this ministry will come back to you many times over.

Name _____
(please print)

Address _____

City _____

State _____   Zip _____

Phone _____(_____)_____

Tear out this page and mail it to:

Norman Robertson Ministries
P. O. Box 10310
Charlotte, North Carolina 28212

ABOUT THE AUTHOR

Dr. Norman Robertson was born and educated in Britain, and in 1974 he moved to South Africa on contract as a professional engineer. Soon after arriving in the city of Durban, he was born again and baptized in the Holy Spirit at a full gospel service. As a result of his personal encounter with the Lord Jesus Christ, he answered the call of God upon his life to study and minister God's Word.

Norman studied and holds credentials with Moody Bible Institute, the Church of God, Rhema Ministries and the Elim Pentecostal Church of Great Britain. He is ordained with Covenant Ministries International and earned a Doctorate of Theology from the School of Bible Theology in San Jacinto, California.

For twelve years Norman was involved in full-time ministry in South Africa and was associate Pastor of a church that experienced supernatural growth to more than 15,000 members. At the Lord's direction he moved to the U.S. in 1992 to be a part of the great revival God is sending to America.

Norman lives in Charlotte, North Carolina, with his wife, Eleanor, and their two children, Jayne and Brian. As a dynamic Bible Teacher, Evangelist and author his anointed ministry stirs and strengthens local churches across the U.S. and Europe. His bold New Testament-style ministry imparts revelation knowledge truth that changes lives and equips the saints. Wherever he ministers the anointing of the Holy Spirit is present manifesting signs, wonders, healings and miracles just like in Bible days.

OTHER BOOKS BY NORMAN ROBERTSON

Winners in Christ

The Supernatural Church

Ministering in the Power of the Holy Spirit

To contact the author, write:

Rev. Norman Robertson
P. O. Box 10310
Charlotte, NC 28212 U.S.A.

It is important to us that we continue ministering to you and helping you to grow spiritually, therefore we are sure you will want to order more anointed teaching materials.

For a complete list of our ministry products — cassette tapes, books, training manuals and videos — write today. God Bless You!

PRAYER CHANGES THINGS

The challenges people face today are genuine and can be very difficult — fears, marriage and family problems, financial needs, depression, struggling with sickness, a lack of wisdom, difficulties in personal relationships and much more. Because we care about people and know the power of God released through prayer changes circumstances, it is the desire of my wife, Eleanor, and me to stand with you in prayer.

Perhaps you are facing difficult situations, discouragement and pressures in your life right now. I encourage you to take action by writing to us and sharing your needs with us. Together, we will release our faith and believe that God will intervene on your behalf!

Let us therefore come boldly to the throne of grace, that we may obtain mercy and find grace to help in time of need.
Hebrews 4:16

Regardless of your situation, take a moment to write and share your special needs with us. When you send in your prayer requests, sow your greatest seed of faith toward your desired harvest. (Luke 6:38.)

Norman Robertson Ministries
P. O. Box 10310
Charlotte, North Carolina 28212

PRAYER REQUEST SHEET

Brother Robertson,

Please pray for the following special needs in my life:

_____

_____

_____

_____

_____

_____

_____
                                              signature

☐ I am enclosing a special seed-faith gift of $_____
and I believe the Lord will multiply my seed sown for the
harvest I need. (2 Corinthians 9:10.)

Name: _____

Address: _____

City: _____ State: _____ Zip: _____

Phone: ____(   )_____

Please make checks payable to Norman Robertson Ministries. All
financial gifts we receive go straight into the Lord's work and are
tax deductible.

Tear out this page and mail it to our address.